COUNTRY INSIGHTS

MEXICO

Edward Parker

RSVP
RAINTREE
STECK-VAUGHN
PUBLISHERS
The Steck-Vaughn Company

Austin, Texas

COUNTRY INSIGHTS

BRAZIL • CHINA • CUBA • CZECH REPUBLIC • DENMARK • FRANCE • INDIA • JAMAICA • JAPAN • KENYA • MEXICO • PAKISTAN

GUIDE TO THIS BOOK

In addition to telling you about the whole of Mexico, this book looks closely at the city of Puebla and the village of Celestún.

This city symbol will appear at the top of the page and information boxes each time the book discusses Puebla.

This rural symbol will appear each time the book discusses Celestún.

Title page: Members of a basketball team from Celestún's secondary school before a game

Contents page: People visiting the Pyramid of the Moon, at Teotihuacan

Consultant: Dr. Tony Binns, geography lecturer and tutor of student teachers at the University of Sussex

Published by Raintree Steck-Vaughn Publishers, an imprint of Steck-Vaughn Company

Library of Congress Cataloging-in-Publication Data
Parker, Edward.
Mexico / Edward Parker.
    p.   cm.—(Country Insights)
    Includes bibliographical references and index.
    ISBN 0-8172-4791-2
    1. Mexico—Juvenile literature.
    I. Title. II. Series.
    F1208.5.P35   1998
    972—dc21   96-52702

Printed in Italy. Bound in the United States.
1 2 3 4 5 6 7 8 9 0 01 00 99 98 97

Contents

Introducing Mexico

Mexico is a country of great contrasts. Within its borders, there are scorching deserts, snow-capped volcanoes, and lush tropical rain forests. Mexico is also one of the twenty richest nations in the world, but, as in nearby Central American countries, there are big differences between the standards of living of the rich and the poor.

Long before the first Europeans arrived in 1519, Mexico was the home of some of the world's greatest civilizations. The best known of these include the Olmecs, the Mayas, and the Aztecs. They built great cities and pyramids, and the remains of many of them can still be seen.

▼ *The pyramids at Palenque are some of the finest examples of Mayan architecture.*

◄ *A farmer from the state of Veracruz*

Tijuana

United States

SIERRA MADRE OCCIDENTAL

SIERRA MADRE ORIENTAL

MEXICO

Monterrey

GULF OF MEXICO

Tropic of Cancer

CARIBBEAN SEA

MÉRIDA

MEXICO

Mexico's place in the world

Mérida

Celestún

Guadalajara

PACIFIC OCEAN

Veracruz

Mexico City
Popacatépetl

Puebla

Pico Orizaba
Orizaba

Villahermosa

BELIZE

Oaxaca

GUATEMALA

N

0   200   400 km

0   200 miles

This book will take you to the city of Puebla and the village of Celestún, as well as the rest of Mexico. You can find these places on the map.

Mexico was conquered by Spain in the 16th century, and Spanish rule lasted for 300 years, until 1821. The Spanish introduced Christianity to the country. Today, 90 percent of the population are Roman Catholics. Spanish is also the main language. But many descendants of the great Mexican civilizations still follow their ancient religions and speak their own languages.

Mexico today is a highly industrialized country. The Mexican people are famous for their high spirits, their spectacular fiestas, and their spicy food, which is now enjoyed by people all over the world.

MEXICO FACTS

Total land area:	**761,659 sq. mi.**
Population:	**94 million**
Capital:	**Mexico City**
Highest mountain:	**Pico de Orizaba 18,700 ft.**
Currency:	**Peso**

Source: *Country Profiles—Mexico 1994-95,*
Economist Intelligence Unit

The City of Puebla

Puebla is a thriving city of more than one million inhabitants, about 100 mi. away from the capital, Mexico City.

Puebla stands close to the site of an ancient Aztec city, called Cholula. Once, Cholula was an important city, but in the early 16th century it was destroyed by the Spanish conquistador Hernán Cortés and his army. Puebla was founded a few years later, in 1531.

▲ *A view of one of the suburbs of Puebla*

During the 16th and 17th centuries, Puebla developed into a wealthy city. It became famous for producing woolen textiles and painted tiles.

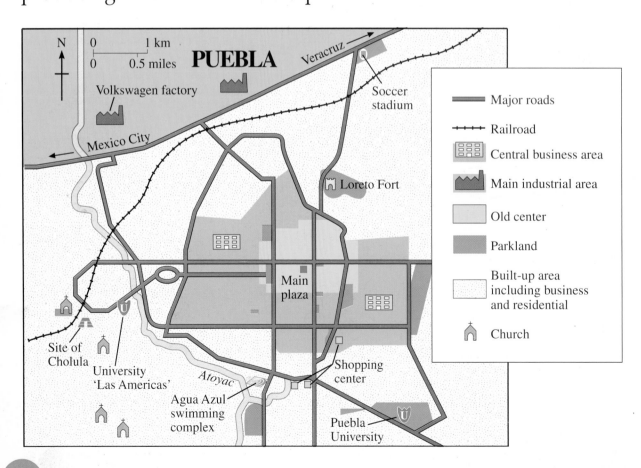

In 1860, the French army of Napoleon III invaded Mexico. On May 5, 1862, the Mexican army defeated the French in a battle at Puebla. There are reminders of this famous battle throughout the city—the main street, for example, is called the Avenue of Heroes. Every year on May 5, fiestas take place all over Mexico to celebrate a great day in the country's history.

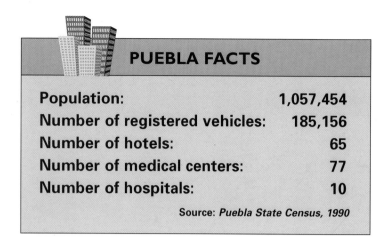

PUEBLA FACTS

Population:	1,057,454
Number of registered vehicles:	185,156
Number of hotels:	65
Number of medical centers:	77
Number of hospitals:	10

Source: *Puebla State Census, 1990*

The people of Puebla are a complicated mixture of the Nahua—who are descended from the Aztecs—and of Europeans. Nine out of ten adults in Puebla speak Nahuatl, the Aztec language, as well as Spanish. Although the Nahua people tend to wear Western-style clothes for work, they still wear their own traditional dress for festivals.

A woman selling strawberries in the center of Puebla

The Village of Celestún

Celestún is a large fishing village with a population of approximately 3,500 people. It lies on the coast of the Gulf of Mexico, on the Yucatán Peninsula. It is about 60 mi. from Mérida, the capital of the state of Yucatán.

The village is built on a narrow strip of land that separates the estuary of the Esperanza River from the ocean. Numerous sandy roads, lined with houses, branch off from the main street. Celestún does not have many old buildings, apart from the church. This is because the village has been destroyed several times over the last 150 years by fierce hurricanes.

▲ *One of the dusty streets in the center of Celestún. Bicycles are the most popular form of transportation in the village.*

Four young children from Celestún ▶

Celestún has a limited number of services. There are three primary schools, a secondary school, and a few shops. The medical center is open only for a few days each week. Villagers have to travel to Mérida if they need to go to a bank or a hospital, and the bus journey takes two hours.

Celestún is in an area of Mexico that has a rich history. More than a thousand years ago, the Mayan people built impressive pyramids and cities in the forests of the Yucatán Peninsula. Links with this great civilization still survive today, as many people in Celestún have Mayan middle names, and older people speak the Mayan language.

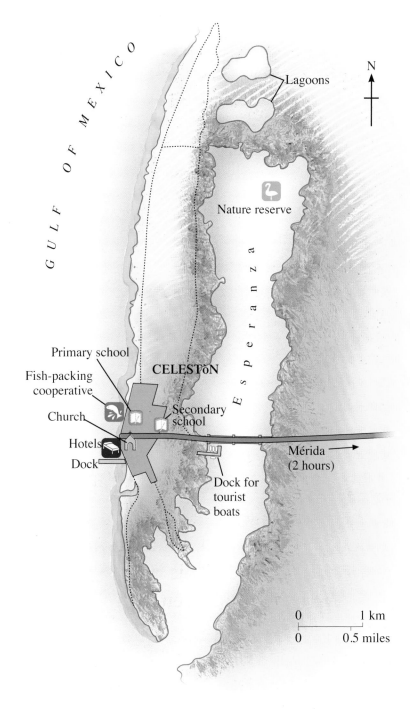

GULF OF MEXICO

Lagoons

N

Nature reserve

Esperanza

Primary school

Fish-packing cooperative

CELESTóN

Church

Secondary school

Hotels

Dock

Mérida (2 hours)

Dock for tourist boats

0   1 km
0   0.5 miles

KEY TO MAP

Houses

Main road

Tracks

Beach

Mangrove forest

Salt pans

CELESTÚN FACTS

Population:	3,500 (estimated)
Number of medical centers:	1 (part-time)
Number of registered vehicles:	39
Number of hotels:	2

Source: *Yucatán State Census, 1990*

Land and Climate

Mexico is a vast country, and it has many different climates. In the north, there is little rainfall throughout the year, and the region has cool winters and hot summers. This area is famous for its deserts and cacti. Much of the central plateau, where most people live, is more than 6,560 ft. high. As a result, summer temperatures are cooler here than in the north. It has a temperate climate, with good rainfall, and these conditions are ideal for agriculture. The southern part of Mexico is tropical, with high temperatures and heavy rainfall throughout the year. Lush tropical rain forests grow in this region.

The main mountain ranges are the Sierra Madre Mountains in the east and west of the country, and the transvolcanic mountain range. Mexico lies along a fault in the earth's crust, so it has had many earthquakes. In 1985, an earthquake hit Mexico City and 8,000 people died. The country also has many volcanoes, and some of them are still active.

▲ The snow-capped Pico de Orizaba, or Star Mountain, is Mexico's highest mountain. Its lower slopes are covered in dense forests.

▶ This cactus grows in Baja California, the driest area of the country, where only 2–4 in. of rain falls each year.

MEXICO'S CLIMATE

Average temperature

	January	July
Tijuana	55° F	70° F
Mexico City	53° F	64° F
Villahermosa	73° F	84° F

Average rainfall

	January	July
Tijuana	2 in.	0 in.
Mexico City	.7 in.	5 in.
Villahermosa	5.5 in.	8 in.

Puebla's Cool Plateau

Puebla is at the southern end of the Mexican High plateau, at an altitude of 7,085 ft. A chain of volcanoes, part of the transvolcanic mountain range, lies just 25 mi. to the south of the city. Several active volcanoes tower above the city itself. One of these is called Popocatépetl, a Nahuatl word that means "Old Smoky."

Puebla has a temperate climate, with good rainfall, and these conditions are suitable for agriculture. Like many Mexican cities, Puebla manages to combine agriculture with modern industry. Corn, beans, and wheat are grown not far from factories producing chemicals, cars, textiles, and electronic goods. There is a good local supply of

The active volcano Popocatépetl can be seen in the distance in this view of Puebla.

clay, which has provided the material for ceramic tiles and plates for several centuries. There is also a large construction industry that uses stone from local quarries.

There are only two main seasons in Puebla: cool, dry winters and warm, wet summers. Even in summer, the temperature can drop quickly when it rains—and after sunset.

The winter months are dry, with warm days and cold nights, although it is not often cold enough for a frost. In and around Puebla there is a large traditional industry making woolen blankets and sweaters. On winter evenings, when the north wind is blowing and the temperature is only a few degrees above freezing, it is easy to understand why this industry has been so successful.

▲ *A farmer and his helper on the outskirts of Puebla plow a field before planting a crop of beans.*

PUEBLA'S CLIMATE

Average annual temperature:	62° F
Average annual rainfall:	39 in.

◀ *Winter mornings can be quite cold in Puebla. These children are wrapped up warmly as they wait for the school bus.*

Hot Tropical Coast

In summer, Celestún looks like a tropical paradise, with its long, sandy beach facing the calm green waters of the Gulf of Mexico. The temperature is regularly more than 95° F, but summer is also the season for heavy rains. Many days begin with clear, blue skies and end in tropical thunderstorms. Several inches of rain can fall in an hour, and then the temperature will become pleasantly cool.

Celestún's climate makes it popular with Mexican vacationers, and foreign tourists have also begun to visit the village. They have been attracted by its beaches and the nature preserve, where there are pink flamingos, crocodiles, and manatees.

CELESTÚN'S CLIMATE	
Average annual temperature:	80 ° F
Average annual rainfall:	30 in.

The main beach at Celestún attracts tourists from the city of Mérida on weekends.

For three months from mid-September, Celestún is in danger from ferocious tropical storms that develop out at sea. Occasionally, a storm turns into a hurricane. In 1995, two hurricanes hit Celestún. Many homes were destroyed, and the entire village was flooded.

Winters in this area are dry, but there is sometimes a cold wind called *El Norte* (the North Wind). When this wind stops blowing, the temperature climbs quickly to more than 86° F, and soon everyone is back on the beaches.

▼ *A fisherman holds a small shark that was caught in one of his nets.*

"In 1995, we had to leave Celestún twice because of Hurricanes Roxanna and Opala.... We stayed in the football stadium in Mérida until the hurricanes had passed.... When we returned home, we found that our house had lost its roof."—Fernando del Angel, 11 years old

15

Home Life

Home life in Mexico revolves around the family. This is a feature that the Roman Catholic and traditional Mexican religions share. It is usual for three generations to live in the same house or at least very near each other. Mexican families enjoy seeing their relatives regularly, and uncles, aunts, and cousins often drop by for a cup of coffee and a chat.

However, in recent years, the pattern of family life has been changing. The average number of children per family has fallen. Young men and women from many families have left home in search of work in the big cities or even in the United States. In some villages and towns, the population is now made up mostly of old and very young people, because so many of the young adults have left.

In Mexican cities, a family with two children typically lives in a small house or apartment, with one or two bedrooms, a living room, a kitchen, and a bathroom. Most houses have electricity and a stove and telephone.

◀ *The girl in the picture is dressed for her first communion. Like most Mexicans, she is a Roman Catholic.*

In small towns and villages, telephones are rare, and firewood is the main fuel for heating and cooking. Baths are not very common in Mexico—most homes have a shower instead. A popular pastime on weekends is to visit thermal springs to bathe with the whole family.

Most Mexican houses are not heated. On cold nights, quilts or extra blankets are put on the beds for added warmth. In the hottest parts of Mexico, people often sleep in hammocks instead of beds.

▲ *Apartments in a typical city street*

THE TORTILLA

Most Mexicans eat tortillas, a type of pancake made from corn flour, with every meal. The traditional breakfast in rural areas is tortillas with meat, beans, and chili sauce. Filled crispy tortillas, called tacos, are popular as a lunch snack in cities and in the countryside. Evening meals tend to be light—perhaps a couple of quesadillas, which are tortillas filled with cheese.

▼ *A typical living room in a house in a Mexican city*

Home Life in Puebla

There are a few apartment buildings in Puebla, but most of the houses are only two floors high. This is partly because of the earthquakes that frequently hit the region, because lower buildings cause less damage than high-rise buildings if they collapse. The houses are usually built of brick or stone, and families live on one level. It is common for grandparents, parents, and children to share the same house or, like the Gomez family, to live next door or across the street.

Nowadays, many women have to do paid work to increase the family income, but they also continue to do most of the housework. They feel very proud to send their husbands and children to work and school each day looking neat and clean.

The Gomez family lives in a house in Puebla. This picture shows them standing outside it, with several of their close relatives who live nearby.

A PUEBLAN SPECIALTY

Puebla is famous throughout Mexico for a special dish called mole. This is a sauce made from chocolate and chili peppers, a mixture that has been popular since the time of the Aztecs. More than twenty other ingredients are also added, and the sauce is poured over meat. Mole is served on special occasions.

▲ *Mole is a special dish from Puebla*

On most days, families eat their main meal together about 2:00 P.M. The children have finished school by this time, and most workers are beginning their siesta. Mr. Gomez works long hours, and often the children are in bed by the time he gets home at night. The two-hour siesta in the middle of the day is a good opportunity for him to spend some time with his family.

▼ *The men of the Gomez family get together for the main meal of the day around 2:00 P.M.*

Like most Mexicans, people in Puebla usually have a late evening meal between 8:00 and 10:00 P.M. This meal is lighter than lunch but still includes tortillas, meat, beans, and chili sauce.

Home Life in Celestún

Most of the houses in Celestún have only one or two rooms. The houses are built of brick, or, more commonly, wood, and each is set in a small, sandy garden where fruit trees and other useful plants are grown. Families in Celestún are generally larger than families in the cities, and over the last few decades the population of the village has grown quickly.

The Pinzon family has a brick house, with just one large room in which they eat, watch television, and sleep. There are no beds, but at night hammocks are hooked to the walls and strung across the room. Cooking is done in an outbuilding, which has an earth floor. Firewood collected from the local mangrove forest is used as fuel.

"There is only one doctor in Celestún and he is only here three days a week. If someone gets seriously injured, their family has to pay 200 pesos ($26) to hire a vehicle to take them to the hospital in Mérida."—Juan Manuel Pinzon, tour guide and fisherman

Hammocks are the best way of keeping cool while sleeping because the network of cords allows air to circulate around the whole body.

▲ *The Pinzon children enjoy a meal of fish, crab, tortillas, and beans after a morning at school.*

Because Celestún is a fishing village, fish is on the menu most days. During the summer, fruit trees provide plenty of oranges, mangos, and coconuts. It is a very healthful diet.

Most families do not own a car, but some of the wealthier families own a moped or small motorcycle. The most popular form of transportation is the bicycle, and almost every family has at least one boat.

Sunday is an important day in the village because the family has lunch and a siesta together.

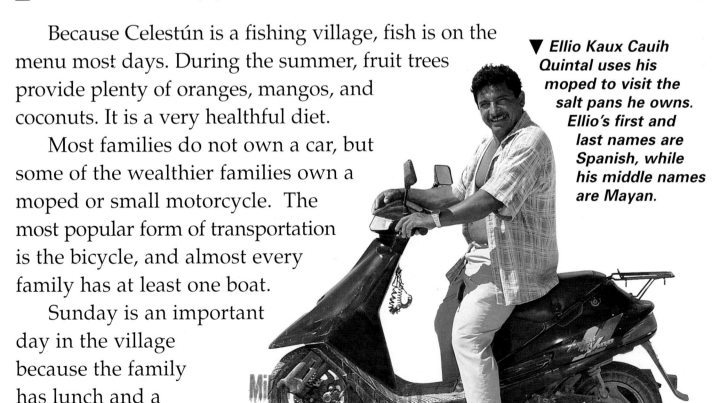

▼ *Ellio Kaux Cauih Quintal uses his moped to visit the salt pans he owns. Ellio's first and last names are Spanish, while his middle names are Mayan.*

21

Mexico at Work

People who live in the United States or Canada are likely to use something made in Mexico every day, although they may not realize it. Many well-known U.S. and Japanese companies own factories in Mexico that make or assemble a wide range of products. These include cars, electrical goods, electronic components, furniture, chemicals, and textiles.

Foreign companies find that it is cheaper to produce their goods in Mexico than to produce them in their own countries. Workers in the car-assembly factories, for example, are paid lower wages than workers doing the same jobs in the United States or Japan. However, conditions in Mexican factories are usually good.

Many other workers are not so fortunate. Large numbers of Mexicans have to work long hours, sometimes in very bad conditions, for very low wages. Others work at several part-time jobs just to feed themselves and their families.

The financial center of Mexico City. The tall buildings are the offices of banks and other major companies.

◀ *A knife grinder at work in the street in the town of Orizaba, southeast of Puebla*

A quarter of all Mexican workers are employed in agriculture. Mexico is famous for producing hot, spicy chili peppers, avocados, tomatoes, and many types of fruit. Fishing is also very important, and anchovies, tuna, and octopus are exported around the world.

Many people are employed in the oil industry, because Mexico is the world's sixth largest oil producer. The country is also the world's largest producer of silver. Other valuable metals mined in Mexico are iron, copper, lead, and gold.

Mexico's natural beauty and its fascinating archaeological sites, such as the spectacular pyramids, attract millions of tourists each year. In 1993, tourism provided jobs for two million people.

TYPE OF WORK IN MEXICO

	Percentage of population (1990)
Services:	51%
Agriculture:	28%
Industry:	21%

Source: *Country Profiles – Mexico 1994–95,*
Economist Intelligence Unit

Many people fish for ▶ *a living in coastal towns and villages. These two fishermen are preparing to set off for a day's work.*

Work in Puebla

People do many different kinds of work in Puebla. Factories produce everything from cars, textiles, and chemicals to processed foods. In the center of the city, there are banks and other financial companies. More than 50,000 Pueblans work for the local government as teachers, administrators, and doctors. Tourism provides jobs in hotels and restaurants. Visitors to the city are also eager to buy goods produced by traditional weavers and potters.

Sergio Gomez works as a taxi driver for one of the many cooperatives in Puebla. A cooperative is a business in which the workers own the company and share the profits among them. Señor Gomez works for five or six days a week and usually for ten hours a day.

TYPE OF WORK IN PUEBLA	
	Number of workers (1990)
Manufacturing industry:	88,000
Commerce:	58,000
Social services:	41,500
Construction:	21,500
Other services:	97,500

▼ *Using a loom to weave wool, which will be used to make blankets*

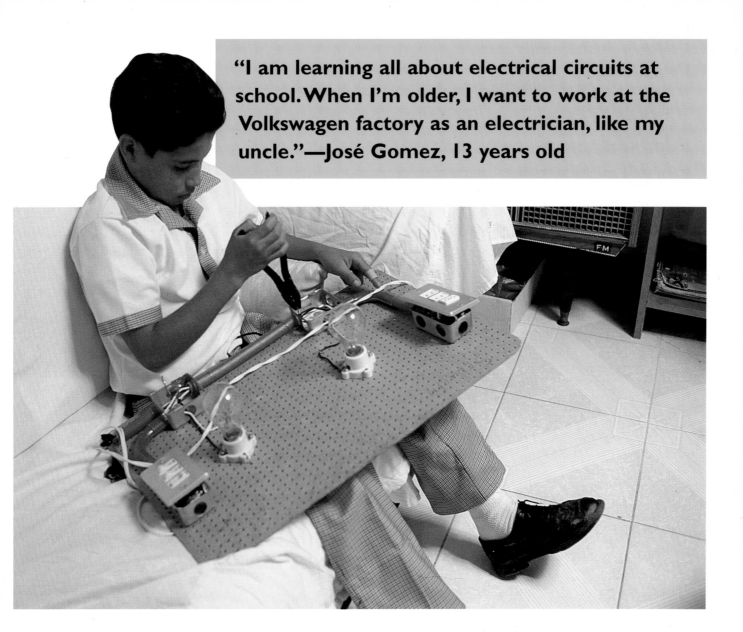

"I am learning all about electrical circuits at school. When I'm older, I want to work at the Volkswagen factory as an electrician, like my uncle."—José Gomez, 13 years old

Sergio's brother, Jorge, works at the Volkswagen factory on the outskirts of Puebla. This factory employs more than 13,000 people—more than any other factory in the city. Most of the 950 cars produced each week are exported to the United States, although some are sold in Mexico. Jorge is an electrician, and he works a forty-hour week, in either morning or afternoon shifts. The working conditions are good, and there are clubs and other activities that employees can take part in once the working day is over. There is strong competition to get a job there.

José Gomez working on an experimental electrical circuit at home

Work in Celestún

In Celestún, the range of jobs available is quite limited. Usually at least one member of every family is involved in fishing.

Juan Mex Quintal usually sets off to sea on Sunday afternoons and spends one or two nights away, depending on how good the fishing is. He cannot go to sea in bad weather, and storms can sometimes prevent him from working for as long as a week.

Juan delivers his catch to one of the fish-packing cooperatives on the beach. There, the fish are sorted and packed in ice. Most go to the city of Mérida, but the more valuable fish, such as yellowtail and lobster, go to the United States. Octopuses are exported to countries as far away as Japan.

Near the village, there are several square miles of natural salt pans, and almost all the families are involved in collecting the salt from them. The salt is shoveled into containers and taken to Mérida to be sold.

Different types of fish are sorted and packed in ice at the fish-packing cooperative.

"It's hot work shoveling salt at the *salinas* [salt pans]... for each ton of salt you get paid about 150 pesos ($20) but it does not take many hours to collect a ton of salt."
—Ellio Kaux Cauih Quintal, former mayor of Celestún, shop and salt-pan owner

◀ *A man working on the salt pans just outside the village*

Tourism has developed quite recently in Celestún and has created more jobs in the few hotels and restaurants. Some people sell shells and other souvenirs; others work as guides on the tour boats. About fifty boats are used to take tourists to see the mangrove forests and the flamingos in the nature preserve. People who fish during the week can earn extra money by working as tour guides on the weekends, because that is when most of the tourists arrive.

A woman selling the many ▶ *different kinds of shells and coral found on the local beaches*

Going to School

Education is considered to be very important in Mexico. The government believes that it is vital to educate young people well, to ensure that the country will be successful in the future. Children are proud to wear the uniform of their particular school.

All Mexican children between the ages of six and fourteen are supposed to go to school. Almost all children enroll at primary school, which is divided into two levels, basic and higher. Each level lasts for three years. Unfortunately, in the countryside, many children leave before they have completed their time at primary school because they have to help their parents on their farms. Other children often have to look after the house and younger children while their parents are working.

Children hold up banners asking for the protection of Mexico's natural environment.

EDUCATION IN MEXICO

In 1991 the average number of pupils per teacher was 30.

87.6 percent of Mexicans can read and write.

In 1990, there were approximately 1.5 million students in higher education.

Only 60 percent of pupils remain in school until they are 11 years old.

More than 50 percent of children enroll for secondary education, for a minimum of three years. Those who want to go to college stay on for three more years, often at special preparatory schools. Pupils are given homework and tested regularly at this stage.

As in most schools around the world, lessons include reading, writing, and math. Mexican schoolchildren also spend a lot of time learning about Mexican history and environmental issues. Pupils are also taught their rights and responsibilities as Mexican citizens.

Sports are considered important. Boys play soccer, baseball, and basketball; the most popular sport for girls is volleyball. Both boys and girls learn traditional Mexican dances.

MEXICO CITY UNIVERSITY

Mexico City University is the largest and oldest university in the Americas. It was founded in 1551 and now has more than 300,000 students. The students often have to take taxis from one lecture to the next, instead of walking, because the university is so large.

Young girls learning traditional dancing at school

School in Puebla

Puebla has 1,165 schools from nursery to secondary level. Between 7:00 and 8:00 A.M., the streets are full of children heading for school in spotless uniforms.

Ruben Ortiz is seven years old and goes to the José Maria Lafrague primary school. Lessons include the history of Puebla and the geography of the local area. Pupils also learn what to do if there is a large volcanic eruption or if another earthquake hits the city. At some primary schools in Puebla, children start taking computer lessons when they are about eight years old.

The two sons of Sergio Gomez attend their local secondary school. This school is in one of the suburbs outside Puebla, and the brothers walk there each day.

NUMBER OF SCHOOLS IN PUEBLA	
Nursery schools:	437
Primary schools:	482
Secondary schools:	246
Universities:	2

Ruben Ortiz in a reading and writing lesson at his school in Puebla

Computer studies is the favorite class of these two children at the Instituto Garcia de Cisneros.

"We start the children on computers in primary school so that they learn to enjoy working with them…. I would say that around 10 percent of pupils at this school have computers at home."
—Martha Salazar, Director of Instituto Garcia de Cisneros

Omar is sixteen and is studying hard because he hopes to enter the famous naval academy in Veracruz. He knows that the entrance examination is very difficult. Omar's younger brother, José, has decided to study electrical engineering at school. He hopes to get a job as an electrician in the Volkswagen factory when he leaves school.

Puebla's two universities have very good reputations, and students come from all over Mexico and from abroad to study at them.

School in Celestún

Celestún has a nursery school, three primary schools, and a secondary school for children up to the age of fourteen. If students want to go on to a college or university, they have to travel to Mérida, the state capital. The bus journey from Celestún to Mérida takes two hours, which is too far for students to travel every day. So they either live in college dormitories or stay with friends or relatives during the week and travel home to see their families on weekends.

The school buildings in Celestún are much more basic than those in the cities, and there are not enough classrooms. The primary school buildings are used by one school in the mornings and by a completely different school in the afternoons. Occasionally, lessons are held outside.

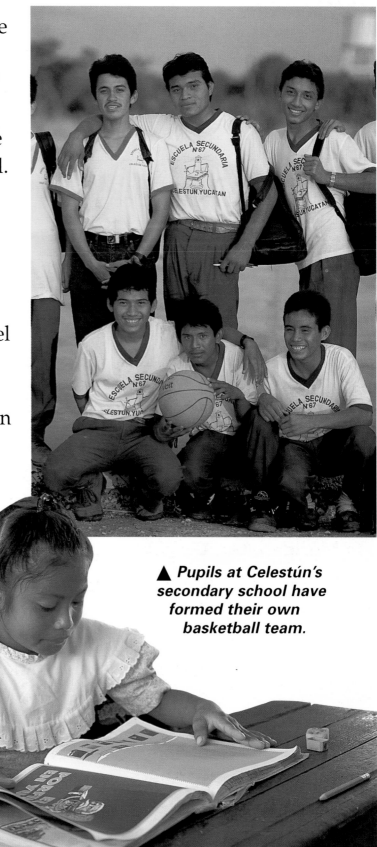

▲ *Pupils at Celestún's secondary school have formed their own basketball team.*

A young girl learning ▶ *about Mexican history in a Celestún primary school*

Primary school pupils read the "wall newspaper," which tells them about World Environment Day.

SCHOOLS IN CELESTUN	
Nursery schools:	1
Primary schools:	3
Secondary schools:	1

"I am studying at the secondary school. I hope to go to a college in Mérida later. On the weekends, I earn money by catching crabs from the river."
– Angel Guadelupe, 14 years old

Children in Celestún do not wear uniforms until they go to secondary school, but the younger ones are always neatly dressed when they set off for school each day. As in all Mexican schools, the day starts with assembly. During assembly, some of the pupils parade the Mexican flag while the national anthem is sung. Children are taught to be very proud of their country.

The children spend most of their time learning reading, writing, and math. There is not much equipment to allow them to carry out science experiments, and there are no computers. Lessons about how to look after the local environment have started recently because natural resources are so important to the future survival of the village.

33

Mexico at Play

Mexicans enjoy sports and fiestas, and they seem to have done so long before Europeans arrived in the 16th century. Near the Mayan pyramid of Chichen Itza, in the south of the country, there are the remains of a ball court with stone hoops on the walls. Here the Mayans played *ollamalitzli*, an early form of basketball, more than a thousand years ago.

Today, the most popular sport is soccer, and almost every town and village has a team. On weekends, people crowd into stadiums such as the Azteca in Mexico City to watch a match. Many people play just for fun in the parks or in the streets. Other popular sports are basketball, volleyball, and baseball.

IMPORTANT HOLIDAYS AND *FIESTAS*

Jan 17	Day of Saint Antonio de Abad
March 21	Birthday of Benito Juárez
April 23	Aztec Day
May 5	Anniversary of Battle of Puebla
Sept 16	Independence Day
Oct 12	Dia del Raza (Columbus Day)
Nov 1–2	Day of the Dead
Nov 20	Revolution Day
Dec 12	Day of Our Lady of Guadalupe

Mexico City's Azteca Stadium, one of the largest in the world, can hold more than 100,000 spectators.

There are many holidays in the Mexican calendar. These are usually held to celebrate religious days or major events in Mexico's history. Some, such as the Day of the Dead, are important for both Roman Catholics and those who follow the older traditional beliefs.

Music is important to Mexicans, and every weekend mariachi bands can be seen playing music in the streets or at parties. Mexicans also like to dance, and many regions have their own traditional dances. On weekends, rock music is played in clubs until the early morning.

Families enjoy getting together for parties. On warm summer evenings, entire families can be seen walking around the parks and plazas together, an activity known as *passeando*.

▲ On national holidays and at religious festivals, Totanac Indians perform ritual "flying." Four men with ropes tied around their waists "fly" from a 33-foot pole. As they swing around the pole, the ropes unwind until the men land on the ground.

▼ Mariachi bands, like this one, play traditional Mexican music.

Leisure Time in Puebla

There is plenty for people of all ages to do in Puebla. It has most of the leisure facilities of a modern city, with shopping centers, theaters, dance clubs, and nightclubs. It also has many historic sites to visit, including the remains of the world's largest pyramid and the Loreto Fort, where the Mexican army fought the French in the 19th century.

▲ The Agua Azul sports complex has a pool that is 16 ft. deep. It is built on one of the natural springs that well up throughout the city.

José Gomez is described as "soccer crazy" by his parents, because he spends most of his time playing in matches or practicing with his friends. His older brother and his father also play for local teams. Puebla has a professional soccer team, too, and sometimes the whole family goes to watch a game in the city's 70,000-seat stadium.

◀ Basketball is one of many sports enjoyed in the city.

When summer vacations arrive and the weather is hot, people crowd into one of the leisure complexes, such as Agua Azul. This has swimming pools, sulfur springs, playing fields, and an amusement park. Puebla's many parks are also full of people walking and playing games, especially on Sundays.

In the summer, the Gomez family likes to go to one of the mountain vacation resorts where they sometimes spend a week in a rented cabin. There, they can enjoy walking in the mountains, swimming in the rivers, and breathing the fresh air. Another popular summer outing is to Africam, a safari park where elephants, lions, and other African animals wander freely around the visitors' cars.

"In the evenings, after I have finished my homework, I like to watch TV or listen to rock music through my headphones."
—Omar Gomez, 16 years old

▼ *Omar Gomez enjoys watching television in his spare time.*

Leisure Time in Celestún

Children spend most of their time out of doors in Celestún, because it is hot most of the year. Soccer is just as popular there as everywhere else in Mexico. In Celestún, it is played in the dusty streets by young children and on the beach by the men who work in the fish-packing cooperative. Girls tend to play volleyball at school and in their spare time.

Most children are good swimmers. Some like to dive off the fishing boats moored by the beach and to collect shells from the seabed. On Sundays and after school, Angel Guadelupe often goes out in a small boat to catch crabs or small fish that his father can use as bait. Fishing provides him with some pocket money, which he spends on drinks or playing games in the arcade. Sometimes he goes to Mérida for a day out.

These boys are enjoying jumping from a fishing boat into the sea.

"There are not many things for children to do in Celestún, apart from riding their bikes or going fishing or swimming…. Sometimes there is a carnival in the town of Hanucuma [one hour away by bus]."—Juan Manuel Ucan Pinzon, 21 years old, tour guide

José Luis enjoys climbing the fruit trees in his garden. He also has an unusual pet—a turtle. In the spring, thousands of turtles arrive at the beach to lay their eggs. Some of the eggs are collected and hatched by the villagers, who keep the baby turtles as pets until they are big enough to release back into the wild.

▲ *Teenagers practice basketball on a Sunday afternoon in Celestún.*

◀ *Girls in Celestún like to play in groups. These girls are playing a card game, where they have to match the pictures on the cards to those on the boards.*

39

The Future

Mexico has many things in its favor. It is one of the wealthiest countries in the world. It is rich in natural resources, such as oil, silver, timber, and fish. It has a young, energetic population and a good education system. It also has a rich and powerful neighbor, the United States. All these advantages give Mexico the potential to develop into an even wealthier and more successful country in the future.

However, Mexico faces many problems as a result of its large population and the growth of its industries. The population is expected to reach 100 million by the year 2000. Mexico City is one of the largest cities in the world, but scientists have predicted that it will be impossible for people to live and work there by 2020 because it is so badly polluted. Pollution is a problem for other cities, too.

◀ *Mexico has many natural resources. This timber is from the forests in the state of Oaxaca.*

▲ *Thick, poisonous smog often hangs over Mexico City.*

Some of the richest people and companies in the world can be found in Mexico, but tens of thousands of people live in very poor conditions in shantytowns around the major cities. The government urgently needs to reduce this gap between the rich and the poor.

There are no easy solutions to the country's problems. But if it can tackle them successfully, the people of Mexico can look forward to a very bright future.

MEXICO'S GROWING POPULATION	
	(millions)
1970	48.2
1980	68.8
1990	81.3
2000	100 (estimate)

▼ *A shantytown in the city of Tijuana, northern Mexico*

The Future of Puebla

Puebla is a thriving city. It is likely to become bigger and more wealthy. However, it may also face problems in the future.

There is a natural danger that threatens the city—the active volcano Popocatépetl, which began erupting again in December 1994. Within the first three days, 8,200 tons of ash had fallen on the valley of Puebla, and 33,000 people had to be evacuated. Fortunately, they were able to return after a couple of weeks. A bigger eruption could have even more serious consequences for the city.

Dr. Alejandro Dominguez uses these photographs of the volcano Popocatépetl erupting to help him in his work.

One of the worst problems facing Puebla is pollution. Fumes from vehicles and some of the large factories produce a poisonous smog that hangs over Puebla for most of the year. Many of the new factories, such as those that make electronic goods, cause much less pollution than the old ones. But Puebla will have to take action to reduce the pollution even more, because there is a danger of the city's becoming seriously contaminated.

Over the last thirty years, new industries have been attracted to the city and have provided thousands of jobs. Despite this, many young people are leaving the area to seek better-paid work in the states of Quintana Roo and Baja California. Puebla needs to continue attracting new employment to ensure that in the future its young people will choose to stay at home.

"Puebla will be the first factory in the world to build the new Beetle [car], from 1998. It is very proud to have been chosen."—Beate Rueck, PR officer, Volkswagen Mexico

The Gomez children hope ▶ to find good jobs in Puebla when they are older, but they also hope that the city becomes less polluted.

The Future of Celestún

Celestún's future will depend on its success in protecting the fragile environment around the village. Fishing is very important to the villagers, but there are many more fishing boats than there were twenty years ago. If too many fish are caught, there is a danger that there will not be enough left to breed, and then there will be no fish for the villagers in the future.

The mangrove forests are very important to the survival of many fish. Large numbers lay their eggs there, and the roots give protection to the small fish until they are big enough to swim out to sea. However, the forest is very sensitive to pollution. An area near the village that is polluted with sewage and trash has already died.

Near Celestún, pollution has already killed some of the mangrove forest.

◀ *Foreign tourists climb into a boat on their way to visit the nature preserve.*

Tourism is important to the economy of the village, but this business could also be damaged if the mangroves and the rare birds and animals in the nature preserve are affected by pollution. The village needs better communications and improved systems for collecting garbage and treating sewage to help it cope with the increasing number of visitors. Such changes would bring benefits not only for the tourists, but also for the villagers themselves.

"After going to college in Mérida, many children return to Celestún, because they can earn a better living as fishermen than they can in other jobs in Mérida…. Only a few children end up leaving the village for good."
—Juan Manuel Ucan Pinzon, tour guide

◀ *Angel Guadelupe catches small fish for his father to use as bait. He will probably become a fisherman like his father.*

45

Glossary

active volcano A volcano that is likely to erupt.

altitude Height above sea level.

conquistador A Spanish word for an adventurer or explorer who goes to conquer another nation.

contaminated Poisoned or polluted with chemicals or radioactivity.

estuary The area of a river where it widens as it reaches the sea.

fault A line of weakness in the earth's crust.

fiesta A Spanish word that means party.

hammock A bed made of canvas or woven string, with cords at each end to allow it to be hooked up.

hurricane A storm with violent winds gusting at more than 75 miles per hour.

industrialized An industrialized country is one that has developed many industries.

manatee A large plant-eating mammal that lives in tropical seas around Africa, the Americas, and the West Indies.

mangrove A tropical tree that grows along coasts and has roots above the ground, rather than underground.

manufacturing The process of turning raw materials, such as steel, into goods, such as cars.

mariachi Bands of strolling musicians who sing and play guitars, violins, and trumpets.

Nahuatl The language of the Nahua people, who are descended from the Aztecs.

plateau An area of high, level land.

resource A supply of something that people can use to survive or make money. Water, wood, coal, and fish are all natural resources.

rodeos Displays of cowboy skills, such as bareback riding.

salt pan A shallow saltwater pool that forms after winter storms. The water dries out in the summer, leaving behind almost pure salt.

services Work such as tourism and banking, which involves providing people with services they need rather than making goods.

siesta A Spanish word for the lunch break, usually taken between 2:00 and 4:00 P.M.

temperate climate A climate that has mild temperatures.

textiles Materials that can be made into cloth.

tropical climate A climate with high temperatures and rainfall throughout the year. This climate is found between the Tropics of Cancer and Capricorn.

Further Information

Books to Read

Chrisp, Peter. *The Mayans*. Look Into the Past. New York: Thomson Learning, 1993.

Department of Geography, Lerner Publications. *Mexico in Pictures*. Visual Geography. Minneapolis, MN: Lerner Publications, 1994.

Irizarry, Carmen. *Passport to Mexico* (revised edition). Passport. New York: Franklin Watts, 1994.

Lewington, Anna. *Mexico*. Economically Developing Countries. Austin, TX: Raintree Steck-Vaughn, 1997.

Reilly, Mary J. *Mexico*. Cultures of the World. Tarrytown, NY: Marshall Cavendish, 1991.

Rummel, Jack. *Mexico*. Let's Visit Places and People. New York: Chelsea House, 1990.

Silverthorne, Elizabeth. *Fiesta: Mexico's Great Celebrations*. Ridgefield, CT: Millbrook Press, 1992.

Useful Addresses

Embassy of Mexico
1911 Pennsylvania Avenue
Washington, D.C. 20006
202-428-1600

Mexican Tourist Office
10100 Santa Monica Blvd.
Los Angeles, CA 90067
213-203-8151

Picture acknowledgments:
All photographs, except page 34, are by Edward Parker.
Page 34: All-Sport Mexico (David Leah)

Map artwork: page 5: Peter Bull; pages 6 and 9: Hardlines
Border artwork: Catherine Parsons

Index

Page numbers in **bold** refer to photographs.